Benedetto
MARCELLO

(1686 – 1739)

Sonata for Treble (Alto) Recorder
and Basso continuo, Op. 2 No. 5
G Major / Sol majeur / G-Dur

Edited by
Manfredo Zimmermann

DOWANI International

Preface

Manfredo Zimmermann, professor of recorder at the Musikhochschule Cologne/Wuppertal and specialist in early music has edited and performed this sonata for treble (alto) recorder and basso continuo op. 2 No. 5 in G Major by Benedetto Marcello. Professor Zimmermann has a very special relationship to this piece of music, since it is the very first sonata which he practised for performance in concert. But even without this personal aspect, the piece is a lot of fun to play.

The CD opens with the concert version of each movement. After tuning your instrument (Track 1), the musical work can begin. Your first practice session should be in the slow tempo. If your stereo system is equipped with a balance control, you can, by turning the control, smoothly blend either the recorder or the harpsichord accompaniment into the foreground. The recorder, however, will always remain audible – even if very quietly – as a guide. In the middle position, both instruments can be heard at the same volume. If you do not have a balance control, you can listen to the solo instrument on one loudspeaker and to the harpsichord on the other. After having practised this piece at a slow tempo, you can proceed to practice both of the *Allegros* at a moderate tempo. We have decided against offering the *Largo* and *Adagio* at a moderate tempo, since both movements are relatively slow in their original versions. Now you can play the piece with accompaniment at the original tempo. At the medium and original tempos, the continuo accompaniment can be heard on both channels (without recorder) in stereo quality. All of the versions were recorded live. The names of the musicians are listed on the last page of this volume; further information can be found in the Internet at www.dowani.com.

As befits its origins, this music relies heavily on elements of improvisation, and we have included only the most essential embellishments and phrase marks. Players are invited to add trills, mordents, slurs and so forth at their own discretion. The same holds true, of course, for the realization of the figured bass (basso continuo or harpsichord), as can clearly be heard on the recording.

We wish you lots of fun playing from our *DOWANI 3 Tempi Play Along* editions and hope that your musicality and diligence will enable you to play the concert version as soon as possible. Our goal is to provide the essential conditions you need for effective practicing through motivation, enjoyment and fun.

Your DOWANI Team

Avant-propos

Manfredo Zimmermann, professeur pour flûte à bec à l'École Supérieure de Musique de Cologne/Wuppertal et spécialiste de la Musique Ancienne a édité et enregistré la présente Sonate pour flûte à bec alto et basse continue op. 2 No. 5 en Sol majeur de Benedetto Marcello. Monsieur Zimmermann a un rapport particulier avec cette sonate, puisqu'il s'agit de la première sonate qu'il a pu étudier et jouer en concert. Mais même sans cet aspect, l'étude de ce morceau procure beaucoup de plaisir et satisfaction.

Le CD vous permettra d'entendre d'abord la version de concert de chaque mouvement. Après avoir accordé votre instrument (plage n° 1), vous pourrez commencer le travail musical. Le premier contact avec le morceau devrait se faire à un tempo lent. Si votre chaîne hi-fi dispose d'un réglage de balance, vous pouvez l'utiliser pour mettre au premier plan soit la flûte à bec, soit l'accompagnement au clavecin. La flûte à bec restera cependant toujours audible très doucement à l'arrière-plan. En équilibrant la balance, vous entendrez les deux instruments à volume égal. Si vous ne disposez pas de réglage de balance, vous entendrez l'instrument soliste sur un des haut-parleurs et le clavecin sur l'autre. Après avoir étudié le morceau au tempo lent, vous pouvez étudier les deux *Allegro*s également dans un tempo moyen. Nous nous sommes abstenu, en revanche, d'enregistrer les mouvements *Largo* et *Adagio* dans un tempo moyen, car les tempos originaux sont déjà relativement lents. Vous pourrez ensuite jouer le tempo original. Dans ces deux tempos vous entendrez l'accompagnement de la basse continue sur les deux canaux en stéréo (sans la partie de flûte à bec). Toutes les versions ont été enregistrées en direct. Vous trouverez les noms des artistes qui ont participé aux enregistrements sur la dernière page de cette édition ; pour obtenir plus de renseignements, veuillez consulter notre site Internet : www.dowani.com.

Cette musique repose à l'origine beaucoup sur des éléments d'improvisation ; c'est pourquoi nous n'avons ajouté que très peu d'ornements et de phrasés. Chaque musicien peut ou doit ajouter ses propres indications (trilles, mordants, liaisons etc.). Cela concerne également la réalisation de la basse chiffrée (basse continue ou clavecin) – comme on l'entend bien sur notre enregistrement.

Nous vous souhaitons beaucoup de plaisir à faire de la musique avec la collection *DOWANI 3 Tempi Play Along* et nous espérons que votre musicalité et votre application vous amèneront aussi rapidement que possible à la version de concert. Notre but est de vous offrir les bases nécessaires pour un travail efficace par la motivation et le plaisir.

Les Éditions DOWANI

Vorwort

Manfredo Zimmermann, Professor für Blockflöte an der Musikhochschule Köln/Wuppertal und Spezialist für Alte Musik, hat die vorliegende Sonate für Altblockflöte und Basso continuo op. 2 Nr. 5 in G-Dur von Benedetto Marcello herausgegeben und eingespielt. Der Herausgeber hat zu dieser Sonate ein ganz besonderes Verhältnis, denn es handelt sich um die allererste Sonate, die er einstudieren und anschließend im Konzert spielen durfte. Aber auch ohne diesen Aspekt macht es großen Spaß, dieses Stück zu musizieren.

Auf der CD können Sie zuerst die Konzertversion eines jeden Satzes anhören. Nach dem Stimmen Ihres Instrumentes (Track 1) kann die musikalische Arbeit beginnen. Ihr erster Übe-Kontakt mit dem Stück sollte im langsamen Tempo stattfinden. Wenn Ihre Stereoanlage über einen Balance-Regler verfügt, können Sie durch Drehen des Reglers entweder die Blockflöte oder die Cembalobegleitung stufenlos in den Vordergrund blenden. Die Blockflöte bleibt jedoch immer – wenn auch sehr leise – hörbar. In der Mittelposition erklingen beide Instrumente gleich laut. Falls Sie keinen Balance-Regler haben, hören Sie das Soloinstrument auf dem einen Lautsprecher, das Cembalo auf dem anderen. Nachdem Sie das Stück im langsamen Tempo einstudiert haben, können Sie die beiden *Allegros* auch im mittleren Tempo üben. Beim *Largo* und *Adagio* haben wir auf das mittlere Tempo verzichtet, da die beiden Sätze im Original schon relativ langsam sind. Anschließend können Sie sich im Originaltempo begleiten lassen. Die Basso-continuo-Begleitung erklingt im mittleren und originalen Tempo auf beiden Kanälen (ohne Blockflöte) in Stereo-Qualität. Alle eingespielten Versionen wurden live aufgenommen. Die Namen der Künstler finden Sie auf der letzten Seite dieser Ausgabe; ausführlichere Informationen können Sie im Internet unter www.dowani.com nachlesen.

Da diese Musik ihrem Ursprung entsprechend sehr stark auf improvisatorischen Elementen beruht, wurden nur die nötigsten Verzierungen und Phrasierungen hinzugefügt. Der Spieler oder die Spielerin darf/soll gerne eigene Ergänzungen (Triller, Mordente, Bindungen etc.) vornehmen. Dies gilt natürlich auch für die Ausführung des Generalbasses (Basso continuo oder Cembalo) – wie in der Aufnahme deutlich zu hören ist.

Wir wünschen Ihnen viel Spaß beim Musizieren mit den *DOWANI 3 Tempi Play Along*-Ausgaben und hoffen, dass Ihre Musikalität und Ihr Fleiß Sie möglichst bald bis zur Konzertversion führen werden. Unser Ziel ist es, Ihnen durch Motivation, Freude und Spaß die notwendigen Voraussetzungen für effektives Üben zu schaffen.

Ihr DOWANI Team

Sonata

for Treble (Alto) Recorder and Basso continuo, Op. 2 No. 5
G Major / Sol majeur / G-Dur

B. Marcello (1686 – 1739)
Continuo Realization: M. Zimmermann

DOW 2521

Sonata

for Treble (Alto) Recorder and Basso continuo, Op. 2 No. 5
G Major / Sol majeur / G-Dur

B. Marcello (1686 – 1739)

DOW 2521

2

II ③

Allegro

III

4

Allegro

Basso continuo

Sonata

for Treble (Alto) Recorder and Basso continuo, Op. 2 No. 5
G Major / Sol majeur / G-Dur

I

B. Marcello (1686 – 1739)

DOW 2521

II

Allegro

III

Adagio

IV

ENGLISH

DOWANI CD:
- Track No. 1
- Track numbers in circles
- Track numbers in squares

1 - tuning notes

- concert version

- slow Play Along Tempo
- intermediate Play Along Tempo
- original Play Along Tempo

- Additional tracks for longer movements or pieces
- **Concert version:** recorder and basso continuo
- **Slow tempo:** The recorder can be faded in or out by means of the balance control. Channel 1: recorder solo; channel 2: harpsichord accompaniment with recorder in the background; middle position: both channels at the same volume
- **Intermediate tempo:** basso continuo only
- **Original tempo:** basso continuo only

FRANÇAIS

DOWANI CD :
- Plage N° 1
- N° de plage dans un cercle
- N° de plage dans un rectangle

1 - diapason

- version de concert

- tempo lent play along
- tempo moyen play along
- tempo original play along

- Plages supplémentaires pour mouvements ou morceaux longs
- **Version de concert :** flûte à bec et basse continue
- **Tempo lent :** Vous pouvez choisir – en réglant la balance du lecteur CD – entre les versions avec ou sans flûte à bec. 1er canal : flûte à bec solo ; 2nd canal : accompagnement de clavecin avec flûte à bec en fond sonore ; au milieu : les deux canaux au même volume
- **Tempo moyen :** seulement l'accompagnement de la basse continue
- **Tempo original :** seulement l'accompagnement de la basse continue

DEUTSCH

DOWANI CD:
- Track Nr. 1
- Trackangabe im Kreis
- Trackangabe im Rechteck

1 - Stimmtöne

- Konzertversion

- langsames Play Along Tempo
- mittleres Play Along Tempo
- originales Play Along Tempo

- Zusätzliche Tracks bei längeren Sätzen oder Stücken
- **Konzertversion:** Blockflöte und Basso continuo
- **Langsames Tempo:** Blockflöte kann mittels Balance-Regler ein- und ausgeblendet werden. 1. Kanal: Blockflöte solo; 2. Kanal: Cembalobegleitung mit Blockflöte im Hintergrund; Mitte: beide Kanäle in gleicher Lautstärke
- **Mittleres Tempo:** nur Basso continuo
- **Originaltempo:** nur Basso continuo

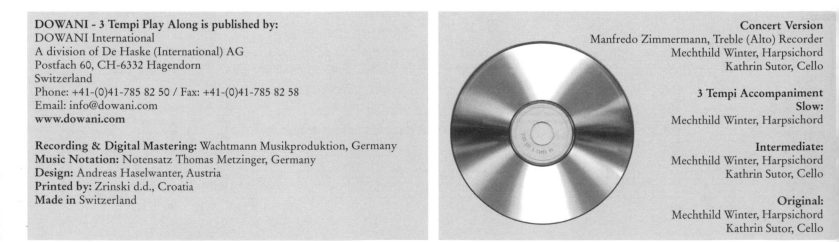

DOWANI - 3 Tempi Play Along is published by:
DOWANI International
A division of De Haske (International) AG
Postfach 60, CH-6332 Hagendorn
Switzerland
Phone: +41-(0)41-785 82 50 / Fax: +41-(0)41-785 82 58
Email: info@dowani.com
www.dowani.com

Recording & Digital Mastering: Wachtmann Musikproduktion, Germany
Music Notation: Notensatz Thomas Metzinger, Germany
Design: Andreas Haselwanter, Austria
Printed by: Zrinski d.d., Croatia
Made in Switzerland

Concert Version
Manfredo Zimmermann, Treble (Alto) Recorder
Mechthild Winter, Harpsichord
Kathrin Sutor, Cello

3 Tempi Accompaniment
Slow:
Mechthild Winter, Harpsichord

Intermediate:
Mechthild Winter, Harpsichord
Kathrin Sutor, Cello

Original:
Mechthild Winter, Harpsichord
Kathrin Sutor, Cello